FREE APP
GRATUITE

AVAILABLE FOR IPAD, IPHONE, IPOD TOUCH AND ANDROID
DISPONIBLE POUR IPAD, IPHONE, IPOD TOUCH ET ANDROID

Scan the QR code or go to
www.amproductions.ca

Numériser le QR code
ou aller à la page web
www.amproductions.ca

Google play   ANDROID

Download Farm Play
for IPad and Android
and Farm Play Lite for
IPhone and IPod Touch

Télécharger Farm Play
pour IPad et Android
et Farm Play Lite pour
IPhone et IPod Touch

KIDS, GET READY FOR AN EXCITING
COLORING EXPERIENCE AT THE FARM.

10 CREATIVE DRAWINGS TO CHOOSE FROM
AND COLOR TO YOUR HEART'S DESIRE.

BUT THAT IS NOT ALL! PRESS THE FUNNY
CAMERA BUTTON TO BRING THEM TO LIFE
AND KEEP ON COLORING!

HAVE FUN!

LES ENFANTS, PRÉPAREZ-VOUS À COLORIER VOTRE
VISITE EXCITANTE À LA FERME!

VOUS POUVEZ CHOISIR PARMI 10 DESSINS
AMUSANTS ET LES COLORIER À VOTRE FAÇON!

ET CE N'EST PAS TOUT! POUR ANIMER VOS DESINS,
APPUYEZ SUR LE BOUTON DE LA CAMÉRA ET
CONTINUEZ À COLORIER!

AMUSEZ-VOUS BIEN!

NIÑOS PREPARENSE PARA UNA EXPERIENCIA
COLORIDA Y ENTRETENIDA EN LA GRANJA.

10 CREATIVOS DIBUJOS A ESCOGER
Y COLOREAR A TU GUSTO.

PERO NO ES TODO! PRESIONA
LA CAMARA COMICA PARA QUE LOS
REVIVAS Y SIGAS COLOREANDO.

DIVIERTETE!

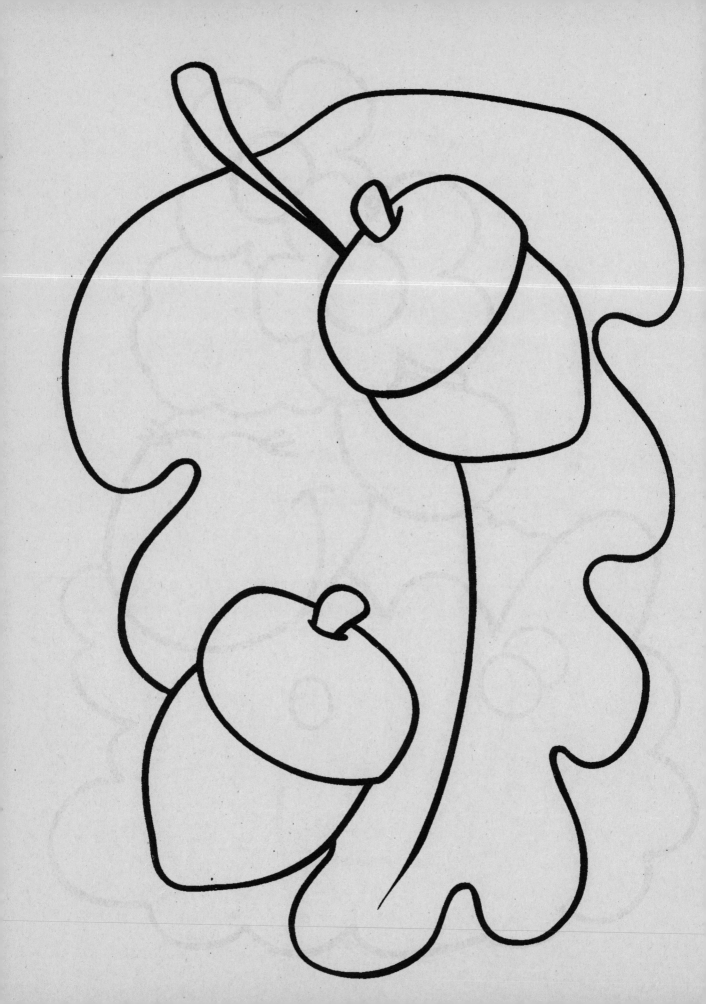

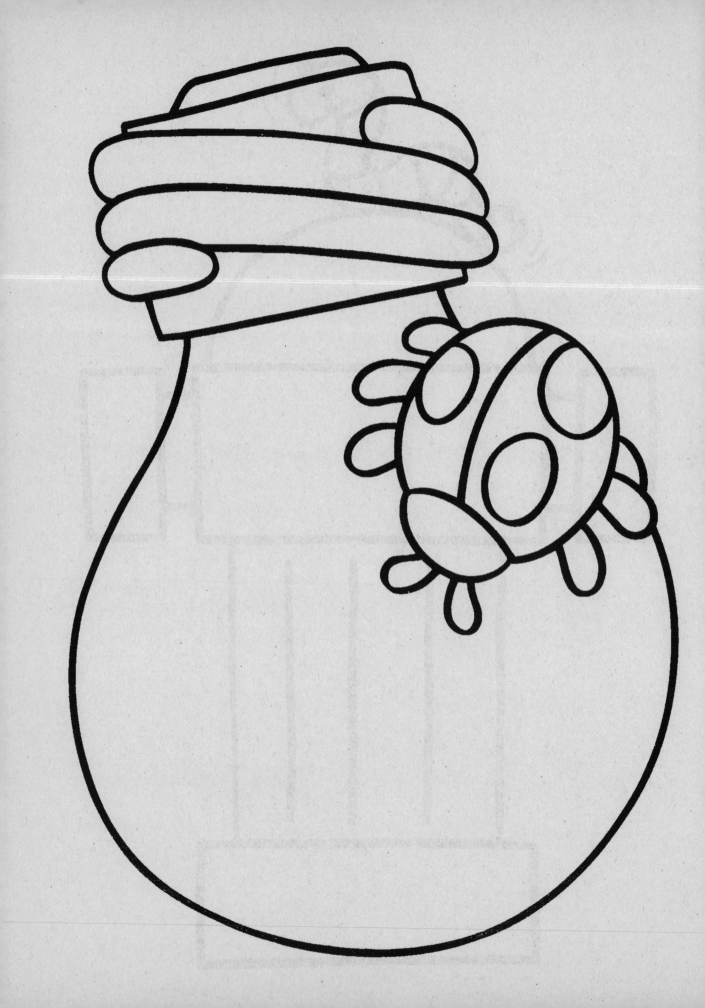

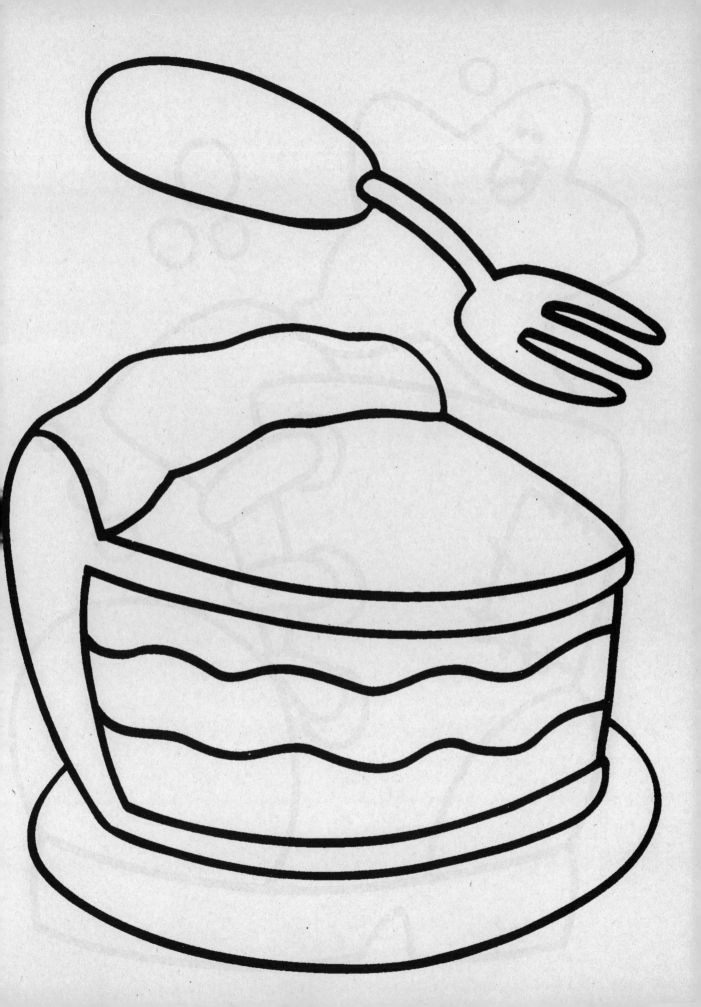

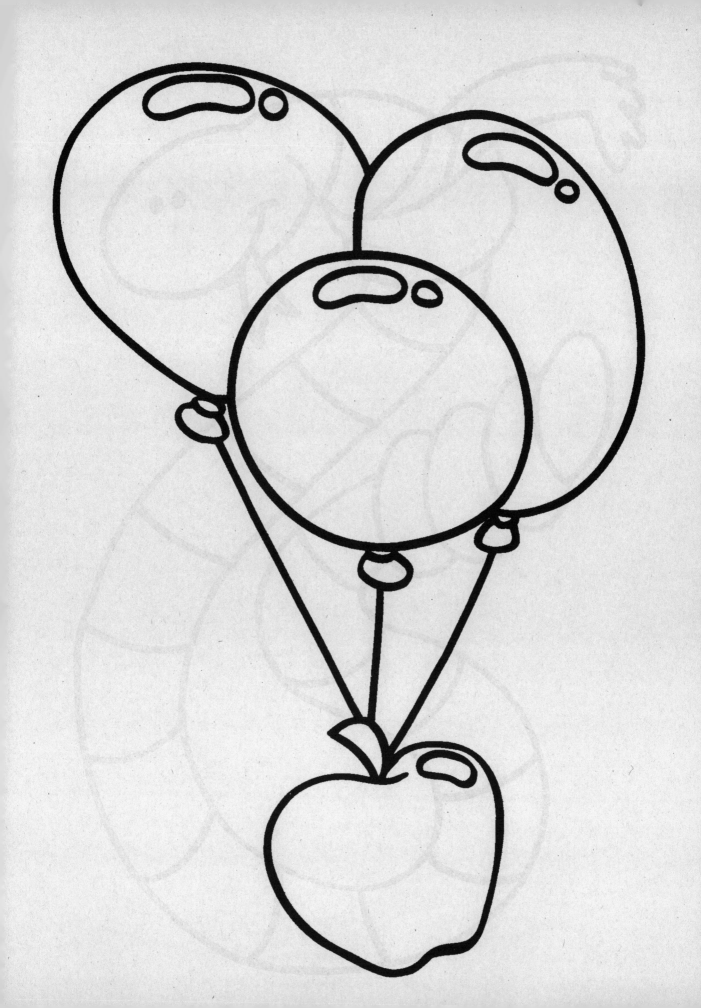

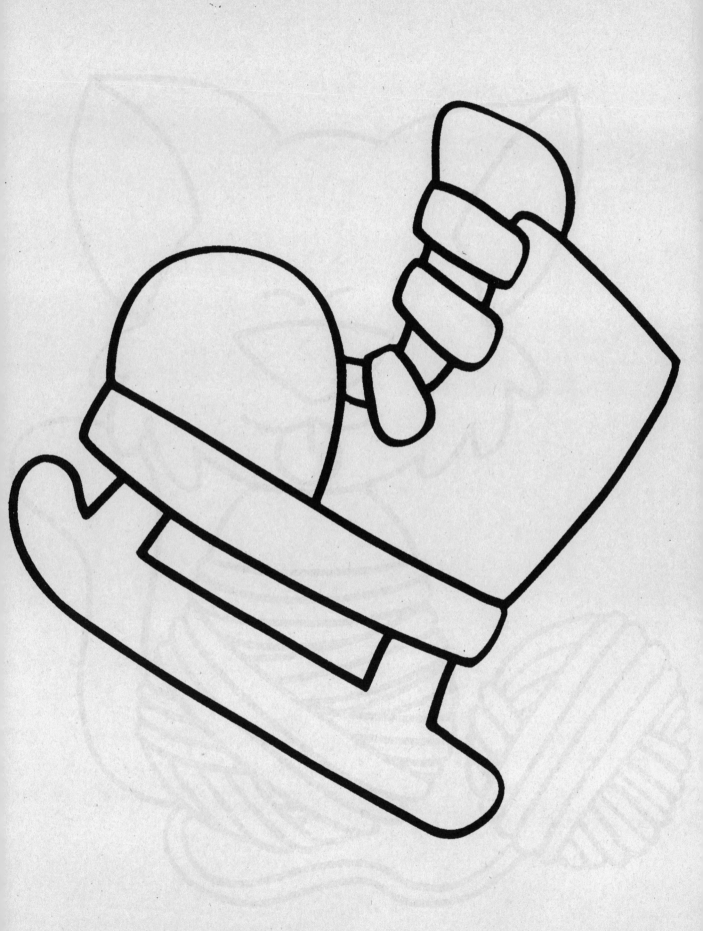

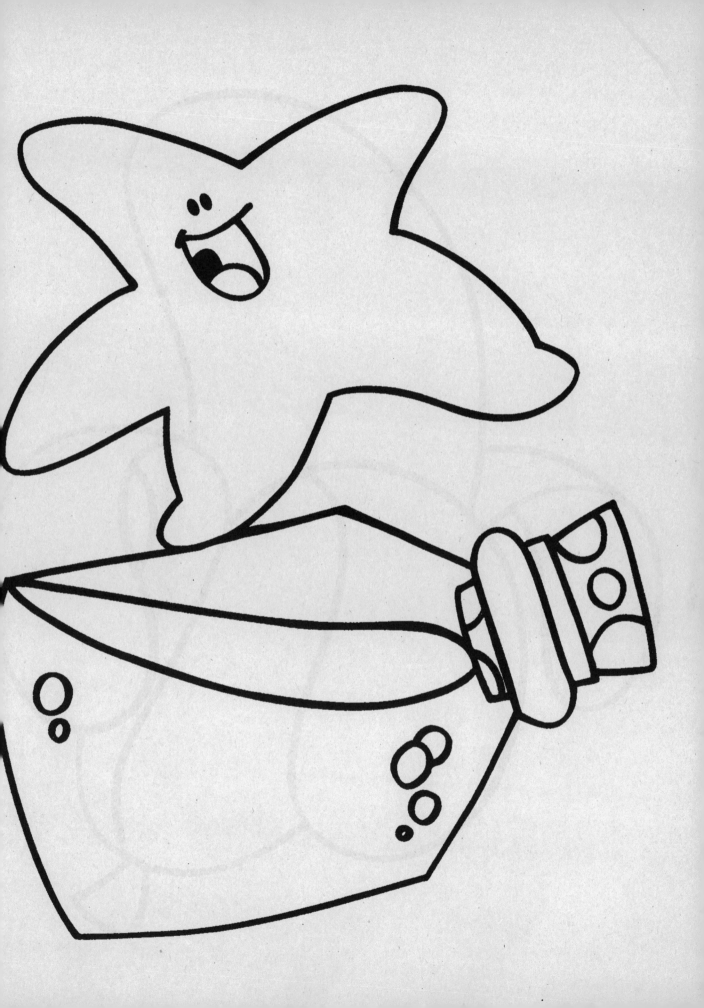

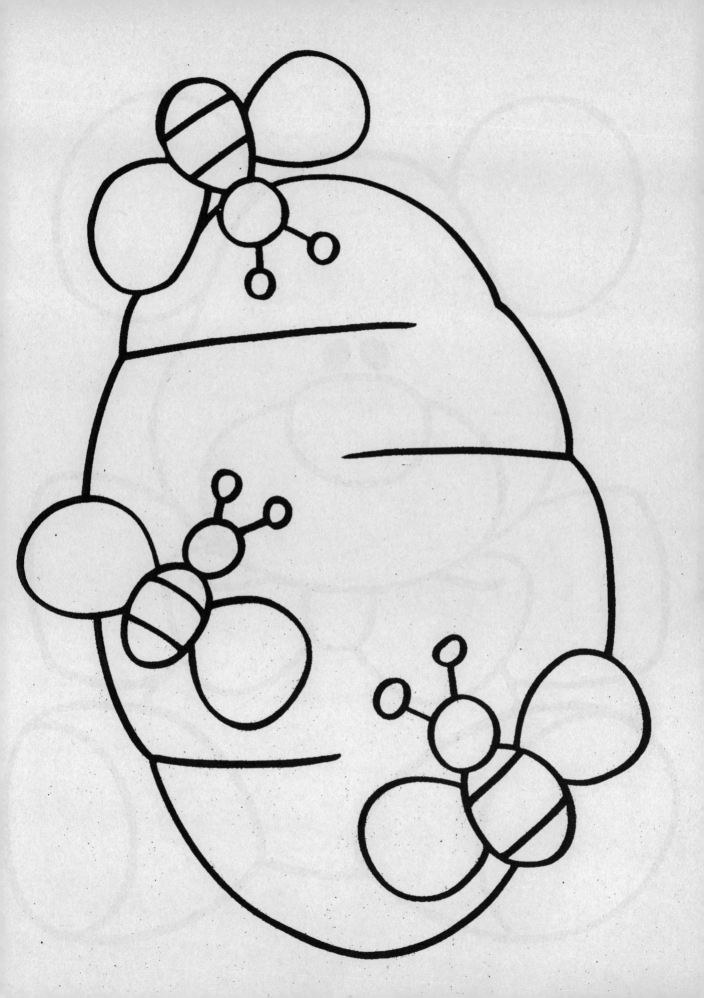

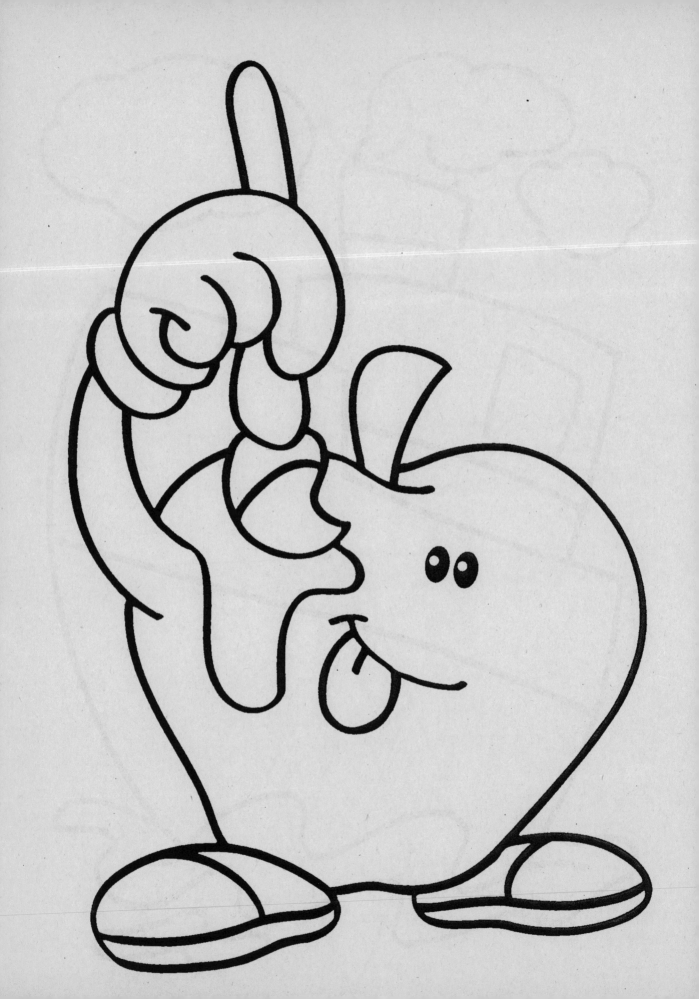